Making the most of mentors and assessors
- Recruitment
- Selection
- Training
- Development

by
Julia Phillipson

Piecing together the jigsaws

Contents

This publication grew out of a project undertaken for CCETSW London and South East England region in 1996–7 to find out more about the recruitment, training and work of mentors/assessors (as defined in CCETSW's Requirements and Guidance for the continuum of social care and social work awards). The project's aims and objectives are given in the Appendix.

Who is it for?

It is written for:

- *individuals* who want to consider becoming a mentor/assessor★ or are already working as mentors or work place assessors and who want to extend this role
- *providers* of education, training and support to mentors/assessors
- *senior managers* and others responsible for integrating organisational objectives, workforce planning and staff development.

How has it been designed?

The text emphasises understanding and building on the potentially significant part that mentors/assessors can play, not only in developing individuals and their practice but also in meeting organisational objectives. Their significance is increased if aspects of their recruitment, selection, training and support are managed strategically and holistically. Each chapter explores different aspects of this process and builds on my own experience of understanding the similarities, the tangles and the fragmentation between different aspects of mentoring and assessment as well as the expertise and experiences of the mentors and assessors I spoke with.

- *Chapter One* sets the scene on how mentoring/assessing is developing
- *Chapter Two* explores the differences and similarities in the titles and roles
- *Chapter Three* provides ideas on recruitment, selection and planning
- *Chapter Four* looks at the training and support needed by both novice and experienced mentors and assessors
- *Chapter Five* emphasises the benefits of developing a strategic approach.

The mix of information, examples, reflections and clues is designed to help further thinking and planning in relation to mentors and assessors.

★ *Chapter Two shows how each part of the social care and social work training continuum "names" their specific role of enabler and assessor to candidates differently. In order to recognise this complexity of naming as well as of the roles themselves the rather clumsy term mentor/ assessor has been used throughout the text.*

Introduction
Curious and curiouser – my journey from mystification to understanding; from curiosity to conviction

Since 1989 there has been a ferment of development across the social care and social work training continuum. New S/NVQs continue to be introduced; competences are reshaped and re-worded; the Diploma in Social Work is established and then changed; the Post Qualifying and Advanced Awards in Social Work and awards for practice teachers and mental health practitioners take on the frameworks, language and expectations of competence; new awards are waiting to "come on stream". Each of these developments has produced its own experts – who may or may not know much about the other areas. Guidance, too, is usually award specific even though the continuum is made up of a series of potentially interlocking jigsaw pieces as shown at the end of *Chapter One*.

Unusually, the initial project was designed to build a broad picture in relation to mentors and assessors. At first I was interested to explore the similarities and differences in the various mentor/assessor roles, to learn what was happening about training and support and to hear people's views on the effectiveness of the training they received. Many of the people I spoke with knew about some awards in great detail while other parts of the training continuum and the expectations of the mentor/assessor were more of a mystery. Discovering sector and regional differences was illuminating as it highlighted the variations as well as the commonalities. My brief also included looking at evidence of strategic planning… and again a very mixed picture was evident.

Later, as I tussled with this rich mix, I came to recognise that although the mentor/assessor role is often but a small part of people's everyday work it is often also pivotal – not only for individuals but also for implementing wider organisational strategies (this resonated with my own experience in a number of mentor/assessor roles). I became convinced of the potential of this pivotal role and that its very contradiction of being both minor in most people's workload and time but major in possible impact is what makes the roles so important.

Before I came to understand the overlaps, differences and apparent contradictions and develop my convictions I met with many questions and concerns, some of which you might also be asking, for example:

Can you explain the difference between a mentor and an assessor to me?

It's not my field – (you'll need to talk to…) should we be considering this?

We're just beginning to develop a corporate strategy about mentoring for managers – we hadn't thought of linking it to the training continuum.

It's all so fragmented...

Why should we bother about mentors and assessors when we are overstretched already; we have to be very clear about priorities – you'll have to convince me...

These comments from staff, training and development providers, senior managers and consortia representatives suggested the differences in awareness and understanding of the roles, the different interpretations of the scope and significance of the roles and the variability in strategic planning in relation to mentoring and assessment.

The comments also generated recurring images for me as people talked – of "fields" – which contained specific expertise, but which often implied high hedges: of "jigsaws" because there seemed to be so many different pieces: of a "maze" as people were sometimes unsure how to find their way around the different awards and roles. And then there were riddles and recipes. These varying images, as well as specific information, appear in the following chapters which attempt to answer the questions and concerns raised and put them in the wider context as well as make some suggestions.

Chapter One
Setting the scene
The wider context and the different jigsaws

In understanding the development of mentoring and assessment, it is important to set it in the wider context of some of the current key features of social care and social work, of social work education and training and to link these to what is happening for individuals.

| **The wider context** | **What's going on for social work and social care organisations?** |

The wider context

What's going on for social work and social care organisations?

Pick up any newspaper, professional journal, or committee report and some themes stand out:

- there is pressure on resources accompanied by a demand for quality
- change in how personal social service organisations are structured and in what they have to do is continuous
- greater involvement of service users, carers and communities is wanted in planning, management and evaluation of services
- inter-disciplinary learning and working is crucial to developing integrated services
- learning, using learning and linking learning to organisational aims is a vital part of survival, managing change and effectiveness.

What's going on in social work education and training?

Social work education and training is changing:

- there is greater emphasis on work place learning, competence and assessment
- occupational standards have been generated that can form a basis for developing and assessing quality standards of practice and management
- clarification of standards is being set alongside a recognition that learning to learn, to reflect on practice and management critically and to use research are all important in a rapidly changing work environment
- a continuum of learning and qualification is in place which aims to ensure consistency of practice for service users as well as development and continuity for workers
- there is an increasing interest in and commitment to developing ways of working and learning inter-professionally and with service users, carers and communities.

What's going on for individuals?

In response to the changing demands, the emphasis on quality and greater diversity of development opportunities:

- there is a very high interest in learning and gaining accreditation or qualifications across occupational groups and at different levels including management

- people want training and development opportunities that are relevant, tailored and valued by the organisation and which include opportunities for sharing, reflecting and applying the learning to a receptive work place and organisation
- however, there's differential access to training and development – for example, residential and home care staff often have less training than other social work staff, black workers often experience particular difficulty in accessing training and gaining promotion; in some regions more women than men are registered for Post Qualifying Awards, while proportionately more men are registered for Advanced Awards.

What's going on in mentoring and work place assessment?

Whilst mentoring in general has a long tradition, in recent times it has become a "growing business":

- each of the social care awards and social work qualifications includes this role as part of the learning and assessment process
- the need to provide mentoring and assessment is often included in job descriptions
- mentors and mentoring are increasingly integral to effective appraisal and career development strategies and processes
- the skills and knowledge required to be an effective mentor/assessor are important for effective management
- management standards include the need to be able to develop teams and individuals to enhance performance
- developments in inter-professional training include inter-professional mentoring
- developing skills and knowledge in mentoring and assessment can now be formally accredited via S/NVQ and the Post Qualifying Awards.

| **The mentor/ assessor jigsaws** | This context of ongoing change, increased expectations of learning and quality places mentors/assessors in a pivotal role of enabling learning and development and of judging standards. As mentoring and assessing has grown a complex jigsaw has developed, as the following examples show. Each award now has its own interlinking mentor/assessor piece as part of its jigsaw of requirements. |

Scottish and National Vocational Qualifications (S/NVQ) have assessors and internal verifiers.

The Diploma in Social Work (DipSW) has practice teachers.

Approved Social Work or Mental Health Officer training in mental health (ASW/MHO) has practice supervisors.

The Practice Teaching Award (PTA) has practice assessors.

The Post Qualifying and Advanced Awards in Social Work (PQSW/AASW) recommend mentors as one important source of learning, support and possibly assessment.

(The planned Post Qualifying Award in Child Care is likely to include an equivalent role, name as yet unknown.)

Individual jigsaws

Some people may be working across a number of these roles – for example, an experienced mental health approved social worker may sometimes act as a practice supervisor and at other times be a practice teacher. Some practice teachers for the Diploma in Social Work may also be acting as a work based assessor for Level 4 in Social Care and so on. Independent consultants may carry a number of mentor/assessor roles.

Equally, an individual may be both a candidate for one award (e.g. PTA) and a mentor/assessor for another (e.g. ASW/MHO) or may be using their involvement in mentoring as part of gaining an Advanced Award.

Inter-professional jigsaws

Shared or joint training is developing between health and social work – including both nurse and occupational therapy training. Shared training for mentors/assessors often accompanies this.

Involving service users and carers in the jigsaws

The role of mentoring and assessment is not confined to professionals. Increasing recognition has been given to involving service users and carers in part of the assessment process, and also as becoming assessors themselves, for example in foster care.

Their jigsaws therefore overlap and extend the other jigsaws.

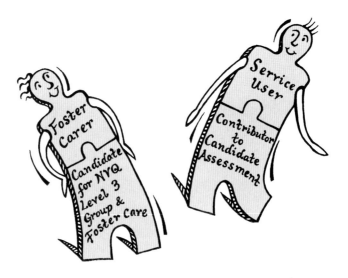

The complete jigsaw currently looks like this

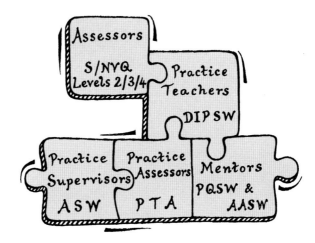

Reflections on the significance of jigsaws

This complexity can, at first, seem confusing or even irritating – why are there so many different names for these roles? What's the difference between them? Is it important to know about all these possible variations? Yes, it is important to see both the separate pieces and the links between them:

- *as an individual* you may want to increase your knowledge of the different awards and see the way these and the accompanying mentor/assessor roles form different pathways and therefore possible routes for role enhancement and career development
- *organisations* can consider the way the different awards and roles can be developed into a mosaic as part of strategic planning linked to organisational objectives and workforce planning
- *training providers* can look at the recruitment, selection and training of mentors/assessors more widely when the links are known about and utilised.

Further reading

CCETSW (1998) *Support to Candidates Undertaking PQ Awards: guidance to PQ consortia*

and each of the relevant CCETSW *Assuring Quality* documents on the different awards.

Chapter Two
What's in a name, what's in the role?

"Come, there's no use in crying like that!" said Alice to herself, rather sharply… she generally gave herself very good advice (though she seldom followed it).

Alice acquired guides and advice givers (mentors perhaps) in her travels through Wonderland in the shape of a caterpillar and a white rabbit, a Cheshire cat and a dodo. Like most of us she found relying on her own knowledge, skills and exhortations was not always enough…

The role of "mentor" has a long and eminent tradition – open almost any book on mentoring and you will find a reference to its origins in Greek mythology. Dictionaries, borrowing from these mythical origins, define a mentor as someone who is an experienced and trusted adviser. Within social work training, as with nurse, occupational therapist, teacher and management training, there has been an increasing recognition of the importance of this role in supporting, advising and guiding learners and workers; hence the view of one respondent that mentoring is "a big industry now".

As learning is increasingly work and competency based the dimensions of judgement, providing feedback and assessment of competence have begun to be incorporated more systematically into the mentoring role as well as into assessor roles. This has been accompanied by the recognition that mentors/assessors themselves need to be more than experienced and trusted and they need to be knowledgeable about and skilled in the processes involved in mentoring and assessment (some of Alice's mentors could certainly have used some training on providing effective and useable feedback!).

As the social care and social work training continuum has been developed and refined the accompanying roles and requirements of mentors and assessor have been sharpened and sometimes extended (e.g. to include observation of practice). The revisions to the Post Qualifying Awards have made arrangements for the provision of a mentor more flexible. This ongoing process of change has resulted in similarities and differences between and within the roles and it is to these that we will turn briefly…

What does a mentor/ assessor do?

"Could I", I was asked as part of the initial project, *"have a look at the similarities and differences in the various roles and see if there was room for a strategic response to the overlaps by CCETSW, by agencies and training*

providers?" …A simple request, surely? As I looked for differences I found similarities, as I looked for similarities I found differences and many variations. And then there were roles with the same name but differences in scope and responsibilities… recollections of Alice's adventures in Wonderland where things were not always what they seemed kept popping into my head. At last the idea of a recipe proved helpful for it is possible to identify some core ingredients in all the roles which can then be mixed with others to taste… or as required!

What follows are examples of different ways of identifying the core ingredients, followed by one or two examples of variations:

1. The essence of mentoring and assessment – simple descriptions

Nixon and McGrath, in their study on supervisors, mentors and consultants in post qualifying training (1995, p10) offer the following descriptions; they say that:

- *mentoring* involves assisting a candidate to prepare for assessment through guidance, discussion, teaching and assisting new learning and reflection on experience and learning. Assessment of learning in a formative sense takes place throughout the process as an educational activity.

- *assessment* involves making final judgements on a candidate's performance, skills, knowledge understanding and values underpinning the area of practice and study. (This is called summative assessment.) In addition, formative assessment is part of the educational process of helping a candidate to consider how much has been learnt, their strengths and other areas still requiring development.

These statements highlight the processes involved, the similarities of the educational element as well as the difference in emphasis and responsibility in relation to formative and summative assessment.

Another way of identifying the ingredients of the roles is to specify tasks and "outcomes". This approach is found in each of the CCETSW award specific documents as summarised opposite:

2. CCETSW requirements of the different roles and tasks

Award	Roles and task of mentors/assessors
Practice Teaching Award *Assuring Quality for Practice Teaching (1996)*	The practice assessor is the person designated by the programme to write a report about the candidate's competence as a practice teacher. Evidence will be drawn from observing the candidate acting as a practice teacher on at least two occasions. The report will provide complementary evidence and overall assessment of the candidate's competence.
Approved Social Work/Mental Health Officer Training The *Paper 19* series *Assuring Quality for Mental Health Social Work* (1996) – England and Wales (1996) – Northern Ireland *Assuring Quality for Mental Health Officer (MHO) Training (1996)* – Scotland	A report based on the observation of the social worker's application of their learning. It would be relevant for a mentor, or tutor and practice supervisor to be in support to guide in the assembly of the portfolios.
Post Qualifying and Advanced Awards *Assuring Quality for Post Qualifying Education and Training – 1 (1997)* *Assuring Quality for Post Qualifying Education and Training (1996) (to be redesignated as Assuring Quality for Post Qualifying Education and Training – 2)*	PQ consortia are required to ensure that candidates have access to people – who may act as mentors – who can: ● disseminate accurate information on the required standards for each of the awards ● advise on what evidence to include in the portfolios and have an understanding of the learning process ● demonstrate a commitment to the values of social work and have up to date knowledge or experience of social work practice.
Training and Development Awards ⋆D32 and D33 for people in assessor roles working with candidates undertaking S/NVQs D34 for internal verifiers D36 possibly for mentors *Assuring Quality for National Vocational Qualifications Awarded by CCETSW (1996)* *Assuring Quality for Scottish Vocational Qualifications (1997)*	Assessors will assess candidate competence by observation and other types of evidence against National Occupational Standards defined by the awards. Internal verifiers ensure verification and standardisation of assessment by assessors across the Assessment Centre.

Footnote: ⋆ *D32 = assess candidate performance. D33 = assess candidate using different sources of evidence.*
D34 = internally verify the process. D36 = advise and support candidates to identify prior achievement.

3. Key tasks

A third approach – my own – is to mix the ingredients of both processes and tasks undertaken on the different awards and to pinpoint the similarities and differences. It looks like this:

A simple description of differences and similarities based on key aspects of the processes and tasks of mentors/assessors

1. Values. As a mentor or assessor you will be required to uphold and demonstrate CCETSW's core values and principles, particularly in relation to anti-racism and anti-discriminatory practice, with candidates and the award programme.

2. The setting for learning and practice. The concept of a "placement" is usually relevant for the Diploma and ASW/MHO training, but not other awards. Work place learning is involved in all the awards, but is undertaken primarily in the candidate's own place of work for S/NVQ, PT award, and for PQ/AASW. Depending on the award and your position you may be in your work place or the candidate's when mentoring or assessing.

3. Developing contracts/working agreements. All awards expect the assessor/mentor and candidates to engage in contracting about their work together, but vary in their expectations of the scope and detail of the agreement.

4. Identifying candidate learning needs is a crucial beginning and ongoing process with the candidate in all awards.

5. Designing a practice based curriculum as well as delivering and evaluating it in relation to the candidate's identified learning needs and the programme's requirements is essential in the Diploma and the ASW/MHO programme, but not on the other awards. All mentors/assessors may help the candidate find different ways of meeting their learning needs – via other colleagues, resources, the Internet, additional practice etc.

6. Scope and frequency of contact. If the candidate is on a DipSW or ASW/MHO placement, practice supervisors and practice teachers will be involved in ongoing and regular contact and may offer weekly supervision. A minimum contact is usually specified by programmes for practice assessors, which is less frequent and usually more dispersed over time. In S/NVQ contact may be determined by the candidate's progress with gaining units and elements, but is best done through regular contact.

7. Observation of practice is required of practice teachers, practice assessors, practice supervisors and assessors. The quantity is limited for the Diploma and the Practice Teaching Award (e.g. two or three times) and is likely to be more frequent in VQ. Direct observation of practice may be required in PQ.

8. Making assessment and judgements are core activities for practice teachers, practice assessors, practice supervisors and S/NVQ assessors.

9. Compiling a report on the candidate is universally expected, though the scope and significance of the report to the overall assessment decision varies.

10. Assisting with portfolio construction may involve all mentors/assessors.

By now, you may have glanced at the jigsaws in *Chapter One* and noticed the differing titles for the mentor/assessor roles; you may also have read the attempts in this chapter to describe what the roles involves. Each of these is both helpful and inadequate as a way of understanding what it might be like to be a mentor or assessor – it is so much more than the lists of tasks and the specifications of requirements…

Core ingredients are not enough

Like all recipes a list of the ingredients of tasks and processes is insufficient – a description of the finished article is crucial, a glossy picture a real bonus. Some understanding of local and individual variations might also be illuminating (think of all the local variations of currant buns – Eccles cakes, Welsh cakes, Bath buns to name but a few). In the course of the project I collected many local differences, for example:

- being on an award yourself and being assessed in your mentor/assessor role seems to generate greater attention on and sometimes time spent with helping the candidate
- programmes running the same award may have very differing expectations of how much time the tasks involved will take, for example being a practice assessor may be thought to take 20 hours or 40 hours – or may indeed take much longer than the programme suggests!
- some programmes expect joint marking of your own candidate's assignments, some want marking of other candidate's assignments, some might ask for reading of other mentor/assessor reports… and so on.

So what's in a role and how is it possible to find out?

The instructions to "eat me" did and didn't do Alice much good… Is there a better way to find out than having to taste it and see… as writer of this text and as a mentor/assessor myself I wondered if I should write some short version of "what it's really like"? Or perhaps I could ask other mentors and assessors or some candidates for their perceptions? None of these seemed very satisfactory so instead here are a few tips and clues for how you might find out more if you want to, followed by some of the reasons why I so enjoy and continue to be enthralled by being a mentor/assessor.

You could:
- read the formal requirements of the role as specified by CCETSW and other relevant awarding bodies
- find out how your local programme or PQ consortium interprets the requirements – most will provide a handbook for mentors/assessors
- read the description of "A day in the life of…" in *Support to Candidates Undertaking PQ Awards* (CCETSW 1998)
- ask someone else who has done it – or two or three people if possible as we all do it slightly differently…
- find out if there's an introductory question and answer session provided by the programme or assessment centre or training departments and go prepared with all of your questions.

What I like about being a mentor/assessor:
- waking up in the morning and realising that I'll be assessing or mentoring for part of the day – a treat
- working with people over time and being part of the ups and down of their learning, their increasing competence – you need a good head for heights and slumps
- seeing not only how individuals change and develop, but how this really improves things for service users (would that new policy on self harm have been developed without the candidate's passion, research and commitment and their being on an award?)
- developing the particular skills of being "at one remove" whilst also staying involved – a curious tightrope
- having to keep thinking about "what's good practice?", both as a mentor/assessor and in relation to the candidate's practice – keeps us both on our toes
- learning from and with each other – so much better than just one head
- going to the award ceremonies – so celebratory and confirming.

… and there's lots, lots more

Reflections on the significance of similarities and differences in names and roles	Exploring what the roles have in common as well as the differences is important because:

Exploring what the roles have in common as well as the differences is important because:
- as an *individual* it may help you recognise your transferable knowledge and skills, or to consider undertaking alternative mentor/assessor roles
- as a *manager* it may be an important consideration in planning for role enhancement or career progression with team members or carers and service users

● as *training providers* identifying the overlaps and differences between the different roles may assist with thinking about widening the pool of potential mentors/assessors for whom the training might be relevant or reviewing the content of the training and support provided (*see the next two chapters*)

● *organisations* may find it easier to consider and plan for the strategic development and deployment of mentors/assessors having recognised the overlaps and may create new avenues as part of positive action strategy (*see the final chapter*).

Further reading

Carroll, L. (1865) *Alice's Adventures in Wonderland* Penguin edition 1998

CCETSW (1998) *Support to Candidates Undertaking PQ Awards: guidance to PQ consortia*

Megginson D. and Pedlar M. (1992) *Self Development – a facilitator's guide* (especially chapter 3) Maidenhead: McGraw Hill

Nixon S. and McGrath S. (1995) *Report of a Preliminary Study of Requirements for Assessors, Mentors and Supervisors in the PQ Education and Training Framework with Specific Focus on Practice Teaching Assessors* Rugby: CCETSW

Pietroni M. (1991) (ed) *Right or Privilege? Post Qualifying training for social workers with special reference to child care* London: CCETSW

Rumsey H. (1995) *Mentors in Post Qualifying Education* London: CCETSW

Novels also often provide different ways of thinking about being a wise and trusted adviser – for example Ann Michaels (1997) *Fugitive Pieces* London: Bloomsbury.

Chapter Three
Who gets to be a mentor/ assessor?
Planning, pragmatism and persuasion in recruitment and selection

Thinking about and planning the recruitment and selection of people into mentor/assessor roles is important for:

● equal opportunities implementation
● meeting the requirements laid down by CCETSW and other awarding bodies
● getting the "right" people into the roles
● creating opportunities for career enhancement and progression for both "obvious" and less obvious people
● linking in to workforce planning and staff development strategies
● as an avenue for carer and service user involvement.

This chapter offers information about what is required and examples of a range of approaches.

What's required	CCETSW is becoming increasingly specific about recruitment and selection of mentors/assessors in its award related *Assuring Quality* papers (see page 13), as shown below.

Award	Selection criteria
Practice Teaching Award	The programme will establish criteria for eligibility to act as practice assessors. Practice assessors will normally be a qualified social worker or allied professional with at least two years experience of practice teaching, staff supervision, post qualifying mentoring or teaching/assessment. It is desirable that they hold the Practice Teaching Award.
Approved Social Work/Mental Health Officer Training	The practice supervisor should have relevant practice experience and understanding and would normally be expected to be a practising approved social worker. They could be the line manager.

Award continued	Selection criteria continued
Post Qualifying Award in Social Work Advanced Award in Social Work	Mentors will need to be able to: ● disseminate accurate information on the required standards for each of the Awards ● advise on what evidence to include in portfolios and have an understanding of the learning process ● demonstrate a commitment to the values of social work and have up to date knowledge or experience of social work practice.
Scottish/National Vocational Qualifications	Assessors who: ● are knowledgeable, competent and experienced practitioners in a relevant branch of care. Internal verifiers who: ● are knowledgeable and competent as practitioners or managers or trainers/ advisors in a relevant branch of care.

CCETSW's Quality Assurance system requires all selection and recruitment approaches to be open and non-discriminatory.

Examples of what happens in practice	**a) Recruitment of mentors/assessors**

A number of different approaches are possible, as the project found, ranging from strategic to pragmatic to serendipitous, for example:

● **strategic** and long term recruitment approaches included writing the role into job descriptions and person specifications as a way of establishing S/NVQs. This was more evident in the voluntary and private sectors and in the residential/home care and special housing settings. It was usually at manager, deputy manager or project leader levels.

● **home grown.** In some agencies involvement with an award or programme over time meant that a pool of expert mentors/assessors was being developed, often built from people who had undertaken the award themselves. The development of "home grown" assessors and mentors was sometimes linked to:

- **succession planning** where individuals were earmarked for progressing from – for example, practice teachers to undertaking the award to becoming practice teaching assessors; or from S/NVQ assessors to internal verifiers.
- **opting out as well as in.** One assessment centre had learnt that it was crucial to provide information sessions so that potential assessors as well as candidates could fully appreciate the implications of undertaking the roles and make an informed choice. This approach, which enabled people to decide not to become an assessor, was reducing fall out and enhancing the completion of awards.
- **proactive targeting.** Some programmes, often as part of an equal opportunities policy, may target certain groups to ensure representation. For example, one PT Award programme requires at least two of the five programme assessors to be Black or Asian. One PQ consortium noted that the majority of its mentors came from child and family backgrounds with few from older people or youth work and is considering with its agency partners the implications and action needed in response to this. In Wales there is an active attempt to recruit Welsh language speaking mentors and assessors.
- **advertising.** Targeting may be accompanied by open advertising e.g. within partner agencies, accompanied by clear role descriptions and criteria for selection.
- **pragmatism, persuasion and local knowledge.** Recruitment often involves keeping requirements in mind whilst mixing them judiciously with being pragmatic. For example, reorganisation might mean more or fewer potential mentors/assessors; having worked with a "problematic" candidate the previous year might mean someone wanted a "breather" and would not be approached. Examples of this mix of local knowledge being blended with pragmatism was particularly noticeable in relation to approved social work where training co-ordinators often had in depth knowledge of whether a person had the needed approach to helping a colleague learn, whether they might have the time and the necessary support from their team and so on. Even so a number of co-ordinators talked of "begging", or even gentle arm twisting of people to become or remain practice supervisors. They often did this with some reluctance knowing the heavy and complex workload of many approved social workers.
- **self selection.** Putting yourself forward to become a mentor/assessor is common and seems to be the result of a mixture of motives and circumstances including interest, wanting to help other colleagues, personal career ambitions etc. One newly "recruited" practice

supervisor explained her decision thus:

The mental health training co-ordinator said "this'll be good for you…". She promotes self development… My team manager is keen for team members to do ASW training and then become practice supervisors – she sees it both as a responsibility and for individual development. As a senior practitioner I am expected to and do offer regular supervision to team members, so this is an extension of that. And I'm interested in developing my own practice and my career…

- **paying – buying in** from outside. Examples of the need to "buy in" mentors/assessors were found across the training continuum where there was a shortage of people with the necessary skills or time. Sometimes this was a short term expedient until more "home grown" people were available.

- **exchanging and poaching.** There were examples of both informal and almost tacit agreements not to poach each others mentors/assessors in some agencies – for example not asking practice teachers to also undertake practice supervision; there were also examples of "borrowing" and poaching from other agencies or other divisions within the same agency – payment could make a difference to people's willingness to be "poached". Some agencies are now in consortia and may exchange candidates and mentors/ assessors.

b) Selection

Again a wide diversity of approaches are possible, some of which dovetail closely with recruitment processes. Examples found in the project included:

- **CCETSW requirements with or without additions.** Where detailed requirements exist – as with the PT Award, programmes generally took these as a basis for selection. Some programmes or agencies might add additional criteria, for example one programme with close links with the voluntary sector specified experience of this sector by practice assessors. Another programme specified that practice assessors must have worked as a practice teacher in the last year to try to lessen the drift from practice teaching to practice assessing as well as to keep practice current.

- **using job descriptions and person specification.** Some programmes and assessment centres are developing and using these. Typically a person specification will detail essential skills and knowledge which go beyond the need to be occupationally competent etc (see for example Gorry Groves chapter 3 and appendix 5).

- **testing for competence.** A range of selection "tests" were found. These included requiring CVs and measuring these against person specifications, interviews or a combination of these. One Practice Teaching Award programme requires potential practice assessors to complete an application form and then demonstrate key skills by watching a video of a practice teaching session as if observing practice. They must then provide written feedback and an explanation of how anti-discriminatory practice would be addressed, as well as judgements about observed competence.

- **licensing.** One assessment centre has developed a licensing system for S/NVQ assessors. This involves attending seven days training, preparing and presenting written material relevant to the O units, answering questions at interview based on the training input, and preparing a Training and Development Award (TDA) action plan. If successful the initial licence lasts for six months. If D32 and D33 are achieved within this time they are then licensed for a further two years. If the D units have not been achieved, evidence of currency of practice and a further action plan is required with an accompanying further six months' licence.

Reflections and questions on recruitment and selection strategies	The range of approaches discovered suggest that diverse strategies are needed to get the "right" numbers and the "right" mix of people available to be mentor and assessors. However, it was also clear that the strategies were often only partially successful. Three aspects appear to be particularly important for consideration – the creating and maintenance of a pool(s), payment, and recruiting service users and carers.

1. Developing and maintaining a pool of mentors/assessors

Common sense seems to suggest that it would be beneficial for there to be a pool of assessors and mentors to draw from and even better that this pool should be strategically managed. This would mean that numbers would be linked to workforce data and planning as well as personal interest; the skills and knowledge of individual mentors/ assessors would be known; the frequency of deployment would be agreed and so on. In developing such a strategy it will be important to consider and ask about:

- **numbers in the pool**
- how many job descriptions include an expectation of mentoring or assessment and at what level?
- how many people are there in each of the award pools currently?
- does this match, or exceed or fall short of the numbers needed?

– what numbers will be needed in the future and what plans are in place to ensure a match of supply and demand?
– have we, or should we have, some reserves?
– have we, at all times, paid attention to the balance of people of particular backgrounds (e.g. race, gender, language) as well as occupational competence?

● **separation, competition and collaboration between pools**

In large organisations, such as social services departments, separate pools of mentors or assessors often seem to develop mirroring organisational divisions. Some settings recruit few people with the necessary qualifications to assess across the continuum (e.g. domiciliary and residential care). There also appears to be growing competition between pools. For example, some practice teachers describe moving out of practice teaching into practice assessing – "it's just as interesting, it's a lot less work and you get paid". The development of S/NVQ Level 4, the new Part 1 of the Post Qualifying Award and the proposed Child Care Award may also put pressure on the pool of practice teachers as the majority are to be found in children and families work. It will therefore be important to ask about and consider:

– are there separate pools of mentors/assessors within the organisation? Are these a result of the award requirements or not?
– in what ways do job descriptions encourage or discourage movement of mentors/assessors?
– what other factors might be resulting in separation and fragmentation?

● **maintaining the pools**

Developing skilled, informed and committed mentors/assessors takes time and resources and it is therefore important to ensure some continuity. Providing time to do the work and to do it well, recognition of its contribution, the provision of support and some reward all seem to be important to maintenance. So it will be important to consider:

– what is known about existing factors which may be assisting or deterring people from continuing as mentors/assessors?
– do some pools have more continuity than others and if so why?
– how might continuity be linked to career enhancement or progression strategies?

2. Payment and other rewards

For a long time many of the mentor/assessor roles have been undertaken as part of existing workload and have received no financial rewards. With the expansion of the roles has come some payments, perhaps prompted further by the use of people acting in a freelance paid capacity. Thus there are some freelance S/NVQ assessors and internal verifiers, but the majority do not get paid, most practice teachers do not get additional payment, but some long arm practice teachers are receiving payment out of the daily placement fee; many practice assessors are paid, at rates negotiated by agencies or programmes. The rates for mentors are often set by PQ consortia – these may be topped up by agencies. The range and amount of payment is important as it affects recruitment and retention of mentors and assessors. Attention will need paying to the repercussions of payment or non-payment as well as to what other rewards and recognition could be considered… thus:

- what is known about who gets paid, how much and for what in the different mentor/assessor roles within and between agencies?
- how is payment affecting recruitment and continuity?
- what other reward systems might be considered?

3. Recruitment of carers and service users

Most of the strategies already outlined have been designed and implemented with employees or freelance professionals in mind. Increasing recognition of the potential of some carers and service users to become mentors/assessors is growing, particularly in relation to S/NVQ or as contributors to practice teaching and the DipSW. Fears of tokenism as well as concerns about whether service users will feel able to offer "truthful" assessments about practice that is not yet competent have slowly begun to be replaced by exciting innovations in working with service users and carers to become familiar with the competences, to provide positive and negative feedback and so on. Agencies and programmes, as well as individual mentors and assessors may want to review, for example:

- what thinking and work has been undertaken so far about involving service users and carers in contributing to assessment or being assessors?
- has enough time been allowed for preparation, training and development of both service users and others involved such as candidates, work based assessors etc.?
- what range of service users and carers are involved?
- what systems and specialist jargon (e.g. recruitment, payments, paperwork etc.) might be deterring some service users from contributing?

Further reading

CCETSW (1997) *Report of a Conference on Working with Service Users in Social Work Education and Training in Social Work and Social Care* London: CCETSW

CCETSW (1997) *Guidance Note 4 for Practice Teaching Programmes: guidance on practice assessment for the Practice Teaching Award* London: CCETSW

Crepaz-Keay D., Binns C. and Wilson E. (1997) *Dancing with Angels: involving survivors in mental health training* London: CCETSW

Gorry Groves S. (1996) *Approaches to the Planning and Evidence Gathering Stages of Assessment* London: CCETSW

For the majority of people, being a mentor/assessor is but a small part of their wider responsibilities. However, it is increasingly recognised that the quality and consistency of work undertaken by mentors/assessors is crucial to a candidate's development and achieving competence and that mentors/assessors too need to develop the necessary skills and knowledge. CCETSW's quality assurance mechanisms recommend that initial training, updating and support for mentors/assessors is provided, but leaves the structure and content design to individual programmes. A number of recent publications provide some award specific recommendations about training and support so here the emphasis is on recognising that:

● recruitment and selection processes will impinge on the nature of the training and support needed and provided

● while initial training is crucial for "novice" mentors/assessors, updating and further training also needs to be planned for and provided

● there may be much greater scope for shared training because of the commonalities in mentor/assessor roles than currently provided.

Project findings

The project found that diverse programmes revealed considerable similarity in training content and structure. This similarity appeared to grow from two key factors:

● some core knowledge and skills is needed by all mentors/assessors

● agencies and often individuals could make only a limited amount of time available to spend on initial training.

Thus, the structure was typically an introductory orientation session followed by one or two days that mixed information giving with opportunities to practice some key tasks and to answer queries and concerns. Such training can be seen as *"enough to get started"*. Further sessions of whole or half days focusing on specific aspects such as evidence gathering or report writing often followed later to coincide with the work actually being undertaken by the candidate and mentor/assessor.

Where programmes recruited people who had already "passed" a competency test such training was unnecessary, although updating sessions might be necessary.

Blending together ideas from different programmes produces an initial core content like this:

Typical core content of the "good enough to get started" introductory training

What's it all about?

Explanation and exploration of:
- VQ/PQ in general and this programme in particular
- competency based education and training
- the value base and anti-racist and anti-discriminatory practice
- who's who and what's where.

What does the candidate have to do and when?

Information and explanation of:
- the award competences
- what the candidate has to "do" to show evidence of competence e.g. tasks, assignments, portfolio construction and submission
- the programme timetable and progress expected.

What do I have to do and how often do I have to do it?

Information and exploration of:
- the role of the mentor/assessor including the role focus and boundaries
- expectation of the role in relation to others such as line managers, tutors, internal verifiers, service users and carers
- frequency and purpose of contacts, other commitments, overall time expectations.

How do I do it?

Information and possible practice of necessary skills or tasks such as:
- contracting and developing working agreements/assessment plans
- identifying learning needs in relation to the award competences
- developing a practice curriculum
- observing practice
- ideas and issues in involving service users and carers in candidate learning and assesssment
- collecting and judging knowledge and performance evidence against criteria
- providing formative and summative feedback verbally and in writing
- compiling a report.

What if?
- identifying and answering questions and concerns
- establishing networking and support systems for mentors/assessors and candidates

Additionally, some initial training might include some of the following:

Exploration of:
- educational philosophies and practice in relation to competency based education and reflective practice
- adult learning theories, models and processes
- anti-discriminatory practice in relation to the role and modelling good practice.

These components are very similar to the idea of a core curriculum outlined in *Interprofessional Education and Training: developing new models* (1996) which clusters the necessary knowledge and skills under three headings: development of self as a practice teacher/clinical supervisor; exploration of adult learning theories, achievement of skills in assessment.

Necessary differences in emphasis

As well as similarities each award has its own emphasis. In S/NVQ more time may be spent looking at different kinds of evidence and issues of currency, validity and so on; practice supervisors may need to consider issues in enabling the learning of and assessing colleagues and peers. Enabling role transition, for example from being an award holding practice teacher to being a practice assessor, may be particularly important for some programmes. PQ consortia may not address practice curriculum design but portfolio compilation and appreciating the difference between the Diploma, Post Qualifying and Advanced Award levels might be crucial.

It will be apparent from these examples that it may be possible and very useful to design some introductory training that addresses core knowledge (e.g. about adult learning and the idea of competence) and core skills (e.g. contracting and providing feedback against competences) for a range of mentor/assessor roles. Some inter-professional Diploma in Social Work programmes already offer this, but few others were found. Why shouldn't practice supervisors and practice assessors learn together? The Practice Teaching programmes may allow automatic credit to TDLB Units 32 and 33 against Unit D Assessment of the Practice Teaching Award so again the framework for joint learning already exists. Introductory training could then be followed up by award specific knowledge and skills as well as support.

Support systems

Handbooks and other written materials are crucial to understanding and undertaking the expectations. A range of other support systems are useful such as those described by Downes and Smith (1991). These include timetabled support meetings, paired support with a more experienced mentor/assessor, regular support from an IV for TDLB assessor candidates; telephone help lines and news updates via newsletters (more common in PQ). These support systems may be closely linked with standard setting and quality assurance. Some programmes also tie payment in with attendance at such meetings, but for most attendance is voluntary and therefore prompts familiar concerns that it is the people who do not attend who often need to!

In undertaking the project it was noticeable how highly valued these differing supports are in offering time to "compare experience and swop stories", trouble shoot, compare reports and "continue to develop the practice of being at one remove". They are valuable not only for "first timers" but also for more experienced mentors/assessors as I know from my own experience.

I recently went to my local support meeting for practice teaching assessors. As usual we worked with both the agenda agreed from the previous meeting and "burning issues" that individuals wanted to discuss. Three hours was barely enough. It set me thinking about my own practice as well as wider issues about the role and its expectations:

● I encourage practice teachers to be creative and try different ways of working with students in supervision sessions – but how much do I model this myself when I meet with the candidate for supervision (must do more)?

● the amount of time spent in the role isn't nearly enough when the candidate is struggling with a problematic student (how much more time can and should be given, and is this then unfair on candidates who have an "easy" student?)

● competence requires evidence of what the individual has done and how they have used their learning – yet much of social care and social work is collaborative – is there a contradiction in this?

Shortly afterwards I read the last chapter in *Mentoring for Science Teachers* (Allsop and Benson 1997) which made me think about whether I could try working with candidates using three different sorts of feedback – evidence of competences, reflective questioning and developmental feedback… perhaps it would be useful to take these ideas to the group?

Approaches to training

The following tables offer an outline of possible different foci for training for mentors/assessors:

Approaches to training for mentors/assessors

	Enough to get started		Complementary	Developmental	
	Novice	*Relevant experience*		*Social work education*	*Career progression*
Assumption/ Starting point	The mentor/assessor has relevant experience and skills but knows little or nothing about the programme and the role.	The mentor/assessor has relevant skills and experience and some knowledge of programme e.g. has been a candidate themself.	Training is unnecessary because recruitment and selection processes are rigorously designed and implemented to assure competence of mentor/assessor.	Person wants to develop their skills and understanding of the role in the context of social work education.	Person wants to develop their skills in relation to wider aspects of current or future role e.g. in training, or in management.
Focus of training	• Provision of sufficient introductory information on the roles, tasks and procedures • *Linking* novice mentor/assessor into the programme • *Emphasising* key issues e.g. ADP; evidence and competence.	• Provision of sufficient introductory information on the roles, tasks and procedures • *Locating* person in their new role as mentor/assessor • *Updating* on changes • Linking to other assessment experience.	• Problem solving and trouble shooting re: mentor/assessor designated issues • Programme development using mentor/assessor's experience • Updating on any changes on awards.	• Extended development of key areas e.g. – adult learning – reflective practice • ADP • Greater focus on mentor/assessor than candidate.	• Further exploration of key areas linked to other roles e.g. – appraisal – personal development plans – mentoring • Focus on different roles of coach, mentor, manager.

Approaches to training for mentors/assessors

	Enough to get started		Complementary	Developmental	
	Novice	*Relevant experience*		*Social work education*	*Career progression*
Assessment/ Qualification	In NVQ assessors will be expected to be qualified with D32 and/or D33 within 18 months of actively commencing the role. Internal verifiers will be expected to qualify within one year with D34.		Where use freelance mentor/assessors some may also have D32 and D33	May be linked to gaining credits for AASW via portfolio or as part of credit rated programme.	Could be linked to MCI or AASW standards and portfolios.
Issues	May be partly used to "weed out" some potential candidates and assessors.	Need to focus on role transition and its implications.

Agencies may feel only limited time is necessary for updating. | May not see "training" per se as relevant. | Necessity?

Time available. | Organisations as well as individuals need to see and promote links between these areas |

Reflections on the significance of different approaches to training and support

New mentors and assessors will need training and support, and this training needs to help them become familiar with what is expected, rehearse and develop the necessary skills and know where to go if problems arise. At the moment the training that is provided appears to be adequate when supported by good written material and support systems.

If mentoring and assessment continues to grow, and with it a pool of experienced mentors and assessors, training and support will need to consider how their skills and knowledge might be enhanced, applied, extended, validated and accredited.

Further reading

Allsop T. and Benson A. (1997) *Mentoring for Science Teachers* Buckingham: Open University Press

Bartholemew A., Davis J. and Weinstein J. (1996) *Interprofessional Education and Training: developing new models* London: CCETSW

Beresford P. (1994) *Changing the Culture* London: CCETSW

CCETSW (1997) *Guidance Note 4 for Practice Teaching Programmes: guidance on practice assessment for the Practice Teaching Award* London: CCETSW

CCETSW (1998) *Report of a Conference on Working with Service Users in Social Work Education and Training in Social Work and Social Care* London: CCETSW

CCETSW (1998) *Support to Candidates Undertaking PQ Awards: guidance to PQ consortia*

Downes C. and Smith J. (1991) *Concerning the Provision, Training and Development of Supervisors and Mentors/Consultants* London: CCETSW

Howe G. (1996) 'Practice in Partnership: working together, training together' in *CAIPE Bulletin.* No 12. Winter: *Involving Users in Interprofessional Education*, pp24-25

"I always knew I could ring up at times of crisis, or when I was in a muddle or just to get straight some of my ideas... I don't know what I would have done without someone to talk to over the years..."

Most of us have had to find a "wise person" we can turn to for advice or guidance or support ourselves, sometimes they have been line managers, sometimes friends and sometimes people who have passed across our personal or professional horizons. Finding this person has been a matter of luck, or determination or skilled and informed searching.

The need for people to be able to find a mentor and act as mentors is becoming increasingly important as change is ever present, as the challenges of practice and management continue to grow and as the time available for developmental supervision recedes. The benefits for organisations are also substantial for skilled mentors can assist with a systematic enquiry into practice, they can suggest new ways to think and talk about "work" and can serve as mirrors to help actions be seen from alternate points of view... (Brookfield p113) Or, like the caterpillar, they can start by asking fundamental questions such as "who are you?" – which Alice found difficult but necessary. Asking fundamental questions such as "what are you here for?", "what were you thinking of?", "why did you work in that way?" continue to be necessary when work becomes pressurised and in danger of routine and short cuts.

Assessors too are vitally important in asking such questions, in working with people to validate existing good practice as well as to develop aspects which currently fall short of expected standards. The need for service users to have skilled and knowledgeable staff who can consistently work in this way continues.

Here are some more arguments for considering developing mentoring and assessment strategically, creatively and economically... just in case some more convincing is still needed.

Arguments for developing mentoring and assessment

The government wants a more competent workforce e.g. 60% to Level 3 and 70% of organisations with more than 200 people to be Investors in People (IIP) registered by the year 2000.	Mentors/assessors are an essential part of helping people achieve competence. Their role is explicitly required for S/NVQ, and the social work awards as well as recommended for management development.
Achieving IIP requires developing systems for supervision, performance review, appraisal and individual development plans.	Recruitment and training of mentors/assessors who can work within and across awards or levels is an important indicator of developing individuals and an organisational learning strategy. Training and support in the skills of mentoring and assessment will complement and enhance skills in supervision, appraisal and learning application.
There are direct benefits for service users, carers and communities when staff are working to explicit and agreed standards – including those of anti-oppressive practice.	Mentors/assessors understand the idea of standards and know how to help and ensure people put these into practice.
Commissioners are increasingly looking at ways of assuring the quality of the services purchased.	The existence of a coherent, implemented strategy of development and training across the continuum is a clear indictor of excellence. Enthusiastic, informed and competent mentors/assessors increase the take up and completion of awards.
The involvement of service users, carers and communities in training and assessment of competence is now recognised as an essential part of ensuring good practice.	Mentors/assessors can ensure that service users, carers and communities are appropriately involved, by actively promoting the value of service user feedback, and ensuring its use. Mentoring and assessment are roles where some service users and carers can be involved in developing not only the practice of individuals but also in developing the team's or the setting's standards of good practice.

Arguments for developing mentoring and assessment continued	
Interprofessional practice and training has been consistently recommended to ensure effective and co-ordinated service design and delivery.	Interprofessional training for people working as mentors/assessors is an important vehicle for developing interprofessional practice.
Black people and women often have less access to ongoing training and development.	Mentoring and assessment can be used for career development and enhancement and as part of training strategies which are designed to counter inequality. Equal opportunities strategies can usefully include formal and informal mentoring.

Turning conviction into action

When Celia Downes and Jenny Smith undertook their study on training and support for mentors and consultants in 1991 they found "no evidence that agencies had begun to establish policies or frameworks related to workforce planning which identified and linked staff training needs within the context of future developments in service delivery" (p8). More recent reports suggest that there is still a scarcity of workforce data analysis and planning (Zutshi) and of a systematic approach to identifying organisational and personal development needs related to workforce planning and organisational effectiveness (OPM). Using both the roles of mentors/assessors that the training continuum creates, as well as the spin offs from these roles in terms of creating a learning culture which is then applied to individual and organisational practice, has great potential.

The project found
- examples of a range of strategic approaches from large scale and long term, to small scale and incremental, broad and narrow approaches
- a tendency to think and plan in "fields" with an accompanying failure to look across and beyond the field hedges and to see the potential for interconnections
- many positive levers that could involve extending the use of mentors and assessors e.g. the increasing use of Investors in People and of CCETSW's Registered Provider scheme, of workforce planning, supervision and appraisal systems, individual development plans etc.

Actual examples include:

Large scale strategic planning
- "we are intending to put in place a continuum ranging from Level 2 to PQ including management Levels 4 and 5, linked to Investors in People, which is a corporate initiative. This has implications for the recruitment, training and deployment of assessors and mentors"
- "as a small authority we realised that we cannot support all these assessor roles, so we are developing a corporate programme on mentoring which is linked to practice teaching and practice teaching competences"
- "two training consultants have been appointed to the department to develop occupational standards across the board. These will result in training and development profiles for every staff member which will identify gaps and plans for how to fill the gaps. These will be linked to the training continuum"
- "we are working with personnel both corporately and within social services to see which jobs and therefore job descriptions should include acting as an assessor or mentor".

Focused and wide ranging strategies
- an authority was prompted into introducing NVQs to "retain provider contracts" which required staff to be adequately trained and qualified. The NVQ systems were initially introduced into one area of service provision and are now being gradually extended into another. Learning from the first experience has resulted in significant changes – e.g. candidates can only register and proceed if there is an assessor on site and agreement from senior management, new assessors have to understand the relevant care awards before learning about the relevant D units. The authority meanwhile is developing personal development plans for all staff which will be developed against national standards.

Award specific strategies
- a small, national voluntary organisation grew their assessor pool by initially deciding to take DipSW students on placement. An interest in practice teaching and then the award developed. A freelance PA was purchased while a senior and social work qualified staff member took the award. This staff member then became a PA for one year while others take the award. This will then be repeated regionally.
- a practice teaching co-ordinator initially recruited a range of in-house practice teachers to act as practice assessors. Concerned about the

variability in standards, she then bought an independent training consultant to act as PA to all award candidates. After gaining the award and continuing to practice teach for a further year staff could then become practice assessors and a support group was set up for them facilitated by the consultant. In this way a home grown pool of assessors was being developed.

A crucial part of developing a strategic approach is to see and plan for the interconnections and to develop jigsaws, for example:

linking people and organisations

linking roles

linking roles to strategies

building in cross overs

Questions senior managers, personnel and training co-ordinators might ask as part of developing strategic planning in relation to mentors and assessors include:

- Are you convinced of the value and potential of mentor/assessor roles?
- Are there any existing systems in the agency/department/ corporately for mentoring which could usefully be linked to the roles on the training continuum?
- Have you used workforce data to identify shortages or surpluses in key areas e.g. domiciliary care, ASW/MHO training or provision and linked this to any plans for recruiting mentors and assessors?
- Are you developing/using existing standards to identify development needs, linking these to personal development plans, the training continuum, mentoring and assessment?
- Have you developed a plan for the recruitment and selection of mentors/assessors which is part of Equal Opportunities; includes the possible use of carers and users, and acknowledges and builds on possible cross overs in these roles?
- Has writing mentoring and assessment into job descriptions been considered?
- Might the range of posts for which this is done be usefully extended?
- Have you an accurate way of collecting information about the numbers and kinds of people in the different mentor/assessor pools?
- Do you know who your current mentors/assessors are?
- Have you a way of monitoring movement across mentor/assessor pools and is this information used as part of workforce planning?
- Do you have a system for succession planning and developing home grown assessors and mentors?
- Have the developments, e.g. of the PQ awards, been taken into consideration in conjunction with workforce planning to identify

the numbers of current and potential mentors/assessors needed?

● Have you developed a multi-faceted strategy for maintaining and developing people in mentor/assessor roles that includes recognition and rewards?

In conclusion

As learning is increasingly work and competence based assessment and judgement of competence are also increasingly required. Developing and sustaining a culture of learning and critical reflection is essential to developing effective, and competent workers and managers and in managing change. That this is neither a luxury nor a sign of failure is already well known. But perhaps what is less recognised and celebrated is the way in which developing mentoring and assessment can be part of this vision and process. It can start small and grow, it can expand outwards as well as up and down (without the need for risking taking bites out of mushrooms or sips of mysterious potions) as hopefully this report has shown...

Further reading

Brookfield S. D. (1987) *Developing Critical Thinkers* Buckingham: Open University Press

Foster G. and Miller C. (1997) *Effective Strategic Management Development for Senior Managers in the Personal Social Services: a commissioning and auditing framework* London: Office for Public Management and the National Institute for Social Work

Megginson D. and Clutterbuck D. (1997) *Mentoring in Action* London: Kogan Page

Zutchi H. (1996) *Workforce Planning Project* London: CCETSW